Searchlight BOOKS™

World Traveler

Travel to

China

Christine Layton

Lerner Publications ◆ Minneapolis

For Mary Louise, Tom, and Roxie

Content consultant: Zhen Zou, PhD, education specialist at the Department of Asian and Middle Eastern Studies at the University of Minnesota, Twin Cities

Lerner Publications Company
An imprint of Lerner Publishing Group, Inc.
241 First Avenue North
Minneapolis, MN 55401 USA

For reading levels and more information, look up this title at www.lernerbooks.com.

Main body text set in Adrianna Regular.
Typeface provided by Chank.

Designer: Mary Ross

Library of Congress Cataloging-in-Publication Data

Names: Layton, Christine Marie, 1985– author.
Title: Travel to China / Christine Layton.
Description: Minneapolis : Lerner Publications, [2022] | Series: Searchlight books. World traveler | Includes bibliographical references and index. | Audience: Ages: 8–11 | Audience: Grades: 4–6 | Summary: "Some of the earliest human achievements took place in China thousands of years ago. Having the largest population of any country, modern-day China is an economic powerhouse. Learn about China with facts, maps, and more!"— Provided by publisher.
Identifiers: LCCN 2021022689 (print) | LCCN 2021022690 (ebook) | ISBN 9781728441665 (library binding) | ISBN 9781728448800 (paperback) | ISBN 9781728444987 (ebook)
Subjects: LCSH: China—Miscellanea—Juvenile literature. | China—Description and travel—Juvenile literature.
Classification: LCC DS706 .L373 2022 (print) | LCC DS706 (ebook) | DDC 951—dc23

LC record available at https://lccn.loc.gov/2021022689
LC ebook record available at https://lccn.loc.gov/2021022690

Manufactured in the United States of America
1-49921-49764-9/2/2021

Table of Contents

Chapter 1

GEOGRAPHY AND CLIMATE

China has an amazing range of landscapes. Dust storms from the Gobi Desert blast across grasslands in the north. To the east, flat plains reach to the sea. China's eastern coastline borders the Yellow Sea and East China Sea. The southeastern coastline wraps around to the South China Sea. In the southwest, bamboo forests hide giant pandas. Mountain ranges and plateaus rise to the west.

Mount Everest, the highest point on Earth, towers in the southwest. Rivers twist through the countryside, connecting the regions of the world's fourth-largest country.

Mount Everest reaches a height of 29,032 feet (8,849 m)!

ZHOUSHAN, IN ZHEJIANG PROVINCE, SITS ON CHINA'S EASTERN SHORE.

China is in East Asia. It borders fourteen countries including India, Mongolia, and Russia. The climate is mixed. Cold winds from Russian Siberia blow across the northern deserts. The seas to the east bring humidity to China's eastern coastline. The south is warm all year long. Mountains make the west cool and dry.

Over half of the land in China is used for agriculture. It is the birthplace of millet and rice. These are two of the world's most popular crops. Farmers began growing millet and rice in China over nine thousand years ago. Chinese farmers also grow wheat, potatoes, cucumbers, and watermelons, among other foods. These crops help to feed the country's population of more than one billion people.

In some areas of China, rice is grown on terraces like these.

Home to a Billion

China has 1,411,778,724 people. About one of every six people on Earth lives in China. Some areas of China, such as big cities, have many people. The city of Shanghai has more than 27 million people. Beijing, China's capital city, has more than 20 million people. Families in cities are usually smaller. Many people live in apartments. Cities provide jobs or other opportunities. Sometimes people move from small villages to big cities for work.

A busy street in Shanghai, China, at night

A village in Anhui Province, in eastern China

Fewer people live in the more rural mountain and desert regions to the west. These regions are home to many of China's smaller ethnic groups. In villages, families tend to be larger. Many people farm and fish. In villages, practicing older cultural traditions is more common than in cities.

Must-See Stop:
Great Wall of China

Millions of visitors come every year to walk the Great Wall of China. The wall is 13,170 miles (21,196 km) long, three times longer than the Nile River. Soldiers, workers, and enslaved people built different sections of the wall over more than two thousand years. Despite its name, the wall is made up of ditches and moats in addition to earth and stone. In modern times, the wall is shrinking. Floods and earthquakes threaten the structure. Some who visit the wall steal bricks.

HISTORY AND GOVERNMENT

The name China comes from the Qin dynasty. Qin Shi Huang united the many kingdoms of China in 221 BCE. He used roads and canals to connect areas together. Before that, many different warring kings ruled parts of the country. The Qin dynasty set up one government, one writing system, and one form of money for the newly united lands.

Historians believe compasses like this one were invented in China as early as the second century BCE.

After the Qin dynasty, each new dynasty added more roads. China's connections grew, and its borders expanded. The country's walls and unified government helped to keep people safe. This allowed Chinese inventors to imagine and create new things. Paper, the printing press, gunpowder, and the compass were all invented in China between 140 BCE and 1100 CE.

The End of Dynasties

For two thousand years, emperors led China. The country survived attacks and wars. But in the 1800s, unrest and famine hit the people of China. China lost two wars to the British and French. People blamed the emperor, Puyi, and those who had been in power before him. Puyi was the last emperor to lead China. The Qing dynasty ended in 1911 when Puyi was overthrown by a revolution. The revolution was led by Sun Yat-sen, the leader of the Nationalist Party. The Nationalist Party succeeded in establishing the Republic of China and in giving control of China to citizens instead of an emperor.

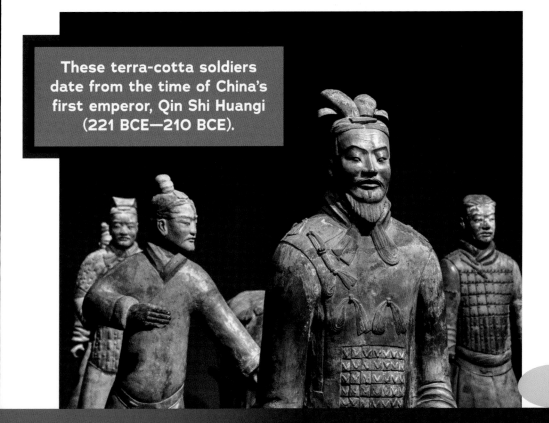

These terra-cotta soldiers date from the time of China's first emperor, Qin Shi Huangi (221 BCE—210 BCE).

Sun Yat-sen became the first president of China. But the struggles did not end. Civil war broke out between the Nationalist Party and another new group, the Communist Party. After World War II (1939–1945), the Communist Party won control of China. The country became the People's Republic of China (China for short). The Communist leader, Mao Zedong, made laws meant to bring the country together. But some policies about farming and food production also led to a deadly famine.

Mao Zedong led China from 1949 to 1976.

President Hu Jintao (*left*) and Premier Wen Jiabao (*right*) led China from 2003 to 2013.

China's next leaders made some changes. They gave more control over agriculture, farming, and food production to the citizens. Under communism, the government owns all businesses and farms. But new laws allowed citizens to make some choices about what to grow. Citizens could also make choices about trade. China's trade suddenly grew very quickly.

The Communist Party continues to lead China. The government owns most businesses, property, and resources. The Communist Party controls the legislative, executive, and judicial branches, as well as the other branches. The National People's Congress is China's legislature. It oversees laws, elections, and China's constitution.

A meeting of the National People's Congress in April 2021

Must-See Stop:
Forbidden City

Visitors enter the Forbidden City through gates 125 feet (38 m) tall. They see the bow-shaped arc of the Golden River, with five white marble bridges crossing it. They then come to a plaza where tens of thousands of people can gather. Above is the throne of the emperor.

The Forbidden City was the center of power in China for over five centuries (1416–1911). After the end of the Qing dynasty, the city turned into a museum.

Let's Celebrate:
National Day

National Day celebrates October 1, 1949. On that date, the civil war between the Nationalist Party and the Communist Party ended and the People's Republic of China began. The day begins with a flag ceremony in Tiananmen Square in Beijing. Some years, a large military parade passes through the square. The day ends with fireworks across the country. National Day is the start of Golden Week, a weeklong holiday.

Chapter 3

CULTURE
AND PEOPLE

China's population is large and varied. At least fifty-six different ethnic groups live in China. The Han is the largest ethnic group in the country. The Han make up 91 percent of the population. Some smaller ethnic groups are the Zhuang, Hui, and Manchu people. All the ethnic groups have their own customs, languages, fashions, and identities.

EACH CHINESE CHARACTER IS MADE UP OF SEVERAL STROKES THAT MUST BE DRAWN IN A SPECIFIC ORDER.

While many ethnic groups speak their own languages, Mandarin is the official language of China. All people must learn Mandarin in addition to the languages they speak in their communities.

Rules for Children

In the 1970s, China's population was growing quickly. The government worried that China could not support so many new people. They made a rule that each family should have only one child. About forty years later, the number of young Chinese people was smaller. Government officials then worried the country would not have enough children. Young people help to take care of older adults. They also take over jobs as older people retire. The Chinese government relaxed the one child rule in 2016.

Even with the one child rule relaxed, many families still choose to have only one child.

Spending time with one's elders is important in China.

In Chinese culture, respect for older people is important. Traditionally, several generations of a family would live together. Grandparents lived with their children and grandchildren. These days, adult children visit their parents and grandparents often. Visits are even required by law. Festivals also celebrate older adults. During the Chongyang Festival, people show respect for everything their elders have done.

Let's Celebrate:
Chinese New Year

Chinese New Year is a festival that lasts for fifteen days. It starts on the new moon that appears between January 21 and February 20. The festival ends on the full moon. People celebrate with fireworks. Many wear red clothes, hang red decorations, and gift money in red envelopes. Red symbolizes energy, happiness, and good luck.

Chinese New Year ends with the Lantern Festival. People hang colorful lanterns, solve riddles, and spend time with family.

Chapter 4

LIVING IN CHINA

Ancient Chinese people invented many technologies. The spirit of invention and advancement is still strong in China. Some of the world's fastest trains connect different parts of the country. China's magnetic levitation trains travel 268 miles (431 km) an hour. The country is also a leader in manufacturing robots. Many Chinese robots manufacture other goods and technologies.

Plans for the future

Many people and resources have helped to make China the world's largest manufacturer. The country makes many products, including footwear, toys, and electronics. It also makes vehicles such as cars and trains. China makes ships, aircraft, space launch parts, and satellites. Other countries rely on China for these products.

A superfast magnetic levitation train travels in the city of Shanghai.

Robotics is a popular area of research for Chinese scientists.

China is growing in trade. The government created a Made in China 2025 national plan. The goal is to make high-quality inventions and products in China to sell to other countries. The plan is meant to transform China from a manufacturing superstar into the top trader in the world.

As the country grows, it also faces challenges. Pollution is one. Burning coal and oil for energy causes carbon dioxide to pollute the air. Untreated waste can also cause water pollution. In 2016, China joined a world agreement to lower carbon dioxide pollution. The Chinese government plans to change from coal and oil energy to natural gas, nuclear, and clean energy.

Wind energy is one type of clean power the Chinese government wants to use.

▲

CHINA HAS A LONG PAST AND BIG CHANGES COMING IN THE FUTURE.

China is a growing world power. The Chinese government wants people to invent more, and for Chinese people to use their own goods. The country is moving into an exciting future. While it is changing quickly, people also honor the past several thousand years of Chinese culture and history.

Map and Key Facts

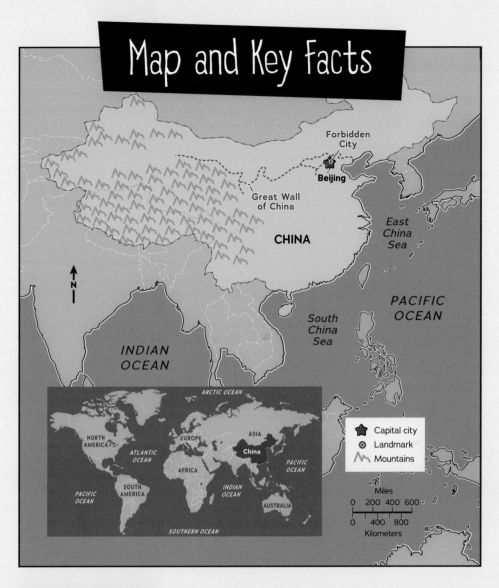

Flag of China

- **Continent: Asia**
- **Capital city: Beijing**
- **Population: 1,411,778,724**
- **Languages: Mandarin, Cantonese, Wu, and many others**

Glossary

agriculture: raising crops and animals

citizen: a person who has full rights in a country

communism: a system where land, property, businesses, and resources belong to the government

dynasty: a series of rulers who belong to the same family

ethnic group: a group of people who share the same country of origin, language, or culture

famine: a serious lack of food in an area

manufacture: create, make, or build

plateau: an area of level ground that is higher than the surrounding areas

revolution: the violent overthrow of a country's government by the people who live there

trade: countries selling and buying goods with one another

Learn More

Aves, Edward. *China through Time: A 2,500-Year Journey along the World's Greatest Canal.* New York: DK, 2020.

Britannica Kids: China
https://kids.britannica.com/kids/article/China/345666

Kenney, Karen Latchana. *Mysteries of the Great Wall of China.* Minneapolis: Lerner Publications, 2018.

Kids World Travel Guide: China
https://www.kids-world-travel-guide.com/china-facts.html

Mattern, Joanne. *China.* Minneapolis: Pogo, 2019.

National Geographic Kids: China
https://kids.nationalgeographic.com/geography/countries/article/china

Index

Photo Acknowledgments

Image credits: Zhengjie Wu/Getty Images, p. 5; Danny Hu/Getty Images, p. 6; Tutti Frutti/
Shutterstock.com, p. 7; Nikada/Getty Images, p. 8; Silvia Campi/Shutterstock.com, p. 9;
aphotostory/Shutterstock.com, p. 10; richcano/Getty Images, p. 12; ShutterStockStudio/
Shutterstock.com, p. 13; Hung Chung Chih/Shutterstock.com, p. 14; AP Photo/Vincent
Thian, p. 15; Xinhua/Zhai Jianlan/Xinhua News Agency/Getty Images, p. 16; Sergii Rudiuk/
Shutterstock.com, p. 17; Shan_shan/Shutterstock.com, p. 18; golero/Getty Images, p. 20;
XiXinXing/Getty Images, p. 21; real444/Getty Images, p. 22; Saigoneer/Shutterstock.com,
p. 23; cyo bo/Shutterstock.com, p. 25; helloabc/Shutterstock.com, p. 26; Haitong Yu/Getty
Images, p. 27; d3sign/Getty Images, p. 28; Laura Westlund, p. 29.

Cover: ABCDstock/Shutterstock.com.